Pobblebonk

My Family

by Dianne Bates

Illustrated by

Jane Wallace-Mitchell

CAMBRIDGE
UNIVERSITY PRESS
www.cambridge.org

This is my family –

Mum, Lib and me, Jill.

We like to sing.

This is my family. Dad and Mum, Ying, and me, Kim.

We like to fish.

My name is Nick and my family is big.

We like to grow chicks.

What is your family like?

What do you like to do?